THE CHILDREN'S BIBLE

Volume 7

A Golden Press / Funk & Wagnalls, Inc. Book
Published by Western Publishing Company, Inc.

Classic™ binding
R. R. Donnelley & Sons Company
patents--U.S. pending
Distributed by Funk & Wagnalls, Inc. New York
Library of Congress Catalog Card Number: 81-81439
ISBN 0-8343-0044-3 (Volume 7)
ISBN 0-8343-0037-0 (12 Volume Set)

CONTENTS

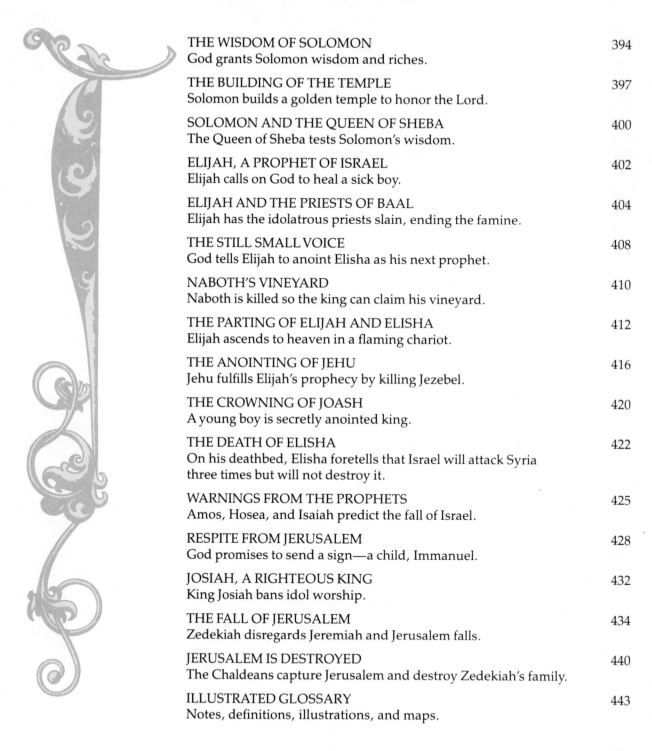

INTRODUCTION

Solomon was king of Israel in a time of peace and prosperity. He strengthened the Kingdom of Israel by building a great army whose soldiers were skilled in the use of horses and chariots. Solomon also made friendships with the rulers of other lands. Many of his wives were the daughters of these kings, so Solomon helped ensure peace with Israel's neighbors by building bonds of family as well as friendship.

Solomon was the richest king ever to rule Israel. He wore robes covered with jewels and ate at tables piled high with many different kinds of food. During his reign, he built a great navy so that he could trade with the people of other lands. His fast ships returned with spices, gold, and jewels from far away, and his merchants even brought back little monkeys to amuse him. Under his reign all Israel prospered and the cities of the nation grew.

Artists, writers, and musicians worked at Solomon's court. Historians wrote down the stories of the nation's past and musicians composed beautiful sacred songs for the temple services. The learned people of Israel wrote religious and poetical works to express their faith in God.

The greatest achievement of Solomon's years of peace and prosperity was the temple he built in Jerusalem. King David had wanted to build a temple but he was too distracted by wars. Solomon's workers began construction on the temple around the year 959 B.C. and finished seven years later. It was one of the most beautiful buildings in the world.

The Israelites believed that God's spirit rested on the temple in Jerusalem. They believed that God was too great to be kept in a temple or to be shown in a statue or a painting. They said that Jerusalem was God's favorite city and that the temple was his favorite home. These were ways of saying that a special friendship existed between God and Israel and that the temple was a sign of that special love.

During the later years of Solomon's reign and in the years following his death, Israel changed in ways that the Bible tells us displeased God. The friendship of Israel's kings with foreign rulers brought strange gods into the land. The people of Israel began to turn all their attention to these false gods and to ignore their own Lord. Solomon and the kings that followed him demanded large sums of tax money from the people, causing hardship throughout the land. The kings forced the Israelites to construct buildings for them and made them join the army.

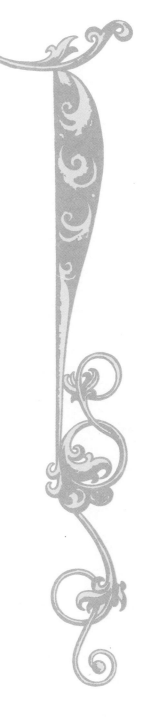

Many people in the nation were rich at this time, but no one cared for the poor or for those without homes. Poor men and women were left to beg for their food.

In these ways many of the people of Israel broke the covenant they had made with God on Mt. Sinai many years before. God had asked Moses and the Israelites to promise to worship him and never to worship the false gods of other nations. God also asked the people to obey his laws, to respect and love one another, and to care for the poor and needy. In the years after David, Israel broke these promises.

God saw the Israelites worship false gods and he heard the cries of the poor and the hungry. He knew that a poor person could find no justice, no shelter, no helping hand in the land of Israel, because his people no longer cared for men and women without power or money. Israel's failure to keep the covenant made God sad. The Bible tells us that God felt like a person who had been hurt by his best friend. Despite his great love for the children of Israel, God punished them so they would be sorry for the way they lived and would change their ways.

God spoke to the people of Israel through the prophets. A prophet is a person sent by God to tell the people that they are offending him and to warn them to change their ways. God told the prophets about his love for Israel and about his sadness that his people had broken their promise. The prophets sympathized with God's sorrow and they became angry because the people displeased God.

When God chose someone to be a prophet, that person's whole life changed. The prophets saw Israel as God saw it. The prophets could not be silent about the injustice and idolatry they saw in Israel. The words just seemed to burst out of their mouths. They had to speak out because they were afraid for the people, and because they knew how much God was suffering because of his people's sins. The prophets knew that God would punish the Israelites, and they did not want the people to suffer. The prophets begged God not to punish his people and they begged Israel to remember the covenant. Traveling through the land, the prophets warned the people to change their lives.

The people of Israel did not listen to the prophets, since they did not like to hear the prophets' warnings. Often the prophets were put in prison or sent out of the cities. So God allowed the powerful Babylonians, Israel's enemy, to destroy his beloved city of Jerusalem. The Babylonians captured many of the people of Israel. The Bible tells us that God had no choice but to punish his people.

from the
BOOKS OF I KINGS
and II KINGS

THE WISDOM OF SOLOMON

A FTER Solomon succeeded his father David on the throne of Israel, he went one day to the holy place Gibeon to offer sacrifice to the Lord, for the temple of the lord was not yet built. And while Solomon was in Gibeon God appeared to him in a dream, saying: "Ask of me whatever I am to give you."

Solomon answered: "O Lord God, I am your servant. You have made me king instead of David my father, and I am like a little child. I do not know how to go out or come in. I am in the midst of your great people whom you have chosen, so great a people that they cannot be numbered or counted.

"Give, therefore, to your servant an understanding heart to judge your people, that I may judge between good and bad. For who is able to judge so great a people as yours?"

God was much pleased that Solomon asked this thing. And God said to him: "Because you have asked for this thing, and have not asked for long life for yourself, nor for riches for yourself, nor for the life of your enemies, but have asked for understanding to make wise judgments, you will see that I have done just as you asked. Lo, I have given you

a wise and understanding heart, so that there has never been anyone like you before, nor shall anyone like you arise after you.

"And I have also given you that which you have not asked, both riches and honor, so that there will not be anyone who is your equal among the kings all your days.

"And if you will walk in my ways, and obey my laws and my commandments, as your father David did, then I will lengthen your days."

Then Solomon awoke and knew that it was a dream. He went to Jerusalem and stood before the ark of the covenant of the Lord, and offered up burnt offerings and peace offerings, and made a feast for all his servants.

SOLOMON GIVES PROOF OF HIS JUDGMENT

Then there came two women to the king, and stood before him.

The one woman said: "O my lord, this woman and I live in one house, and I bore a child in the house with her. And it happened that three days afterward, this woman bore a child too. We were together, and there was no one else in the house with the two of us.

"This woman's child died in the night and she arose at midnight and took my son from beside me, while your handmaid slept, and she took him in her arms and laid her dead child in my arms.

"And when I rose in the morning to nurse my child, I saw that it was dead. But when I had looked at it in the daylight, I found that it was not my own son."

The other woman said: "No, the living is my son, and the dead is your son."

And the first woman said: "No, the dead is your son and the living is my son."

Thus they argued before the king.

Then the king said:

"The one says, 'This is my son that is alive, and your son is the dead child,' the other says, 'No, your son is the dead one, and my son is the living.'" So the king said: "Bring me a sword." And they brought him a sword. "Divide the living child in two," he said, "and give half to the one and half to the other."

Then the mother to whom the living child belonged spoke to the king, for her heart ached for her son, and she said: "O Lord, give her the living child, but by no means kill it."

But the other said: "Let it be neither mine nor yours, but divide it."

Then the king answered and said: "Give the first woman the living child, and by no means kill it. She is the mother of it."

All Israel heard of the judgment which the king had handed down, and they respected the king. For they saw that the wisdom of God was in him, to give judgments.

And God gave Solomon great wisdom and understanding, and largeness of heart as the sand that is on the seashore. And Solomon's wisdom excelled the wisdom of all the children of the east country and all the wisdom of Egypt. For he was wiser than all men, and his fame spread through all nations round about.

THE BUILDING OF THE TEMPLE

OW in the four hundred and eightieth year after the children of Israel had come out of the land of Egypt, Solomon, in the fourth year of his reign, began to build a temple to the Lord.

The house of the Lord which king Solomon built was ninety feet long and thirty feet broad, and the height of it was forty-five feet. There was a broad porch before the temple, and it had windows of narrow lights, and many chambers.

The house was built of stone made ready before it was brought there, so that there was no sound of a hammer or ax or any tool in the house while it was being built.

The walls and floors and ceilings of the house were of boards of cedar, and Solomon covered the floors with planks of fir.

And he covered the whole house with pure gold, and the whole altar in the holy of holies was covered with pure gold. Within the holy of holies he had two cherubim of olive wood, each fifteen feet high, and their wings touched in the middle of the room. They too were overlaid with gold.

All the walls and the doors were carved with cherubim and with palm trees and flowers, all covered with gold, and in the inner court were three rows of hewed stone columns, and a row of cedar beams.

Solomon caused all the vessels that belonged to the house of the Lord to be made of gold likewise. The altar was of gold, and the candlesticks of pure gold, before the holy of holies, with flowers and lamps and tongs of gold; and bowls and snuffers and basins and spoons and censers of pure gold, and hinges of gold on the doors of the temple.

The house was seven years in the building. Then the work was finished which king Solomon had done for the house of the Lord. And Solomon brought in the things which David his father had dedicated. The silver and the gold and the vessels he put among the treasures of the house of the Lord.

Then Solomon assembled the elders of Israel and all the heads of the tribes, that they might bring the ark of the Lord's covenant into the temple at Jerusalem.

The priests brought the ark of the

covenant into the holy of holies, under the spread wings of the cherubim. There was nothing in the ark except the two tablets of stone which Moses had put there at Horeb when the Lord made a covenant with the children of Israel when they came out of the land of Egypt.

And it came to pass, when the priests had come out of the holy place, that a cloud filled the house of the Lord, so that the priests could not stand to minister, because of the glory of the Lord which filled the house of the Lord.

And Solomon blessed all the congregation of Israel and said:

"Blessed be the Lord God of Israel. I have built a house for the Lord and have set there a place for the ark wherein is the covenant of the Lord, which he made with our fathers, in the days when he brought them out of the land of Egypt."

399

SOLOMON AND THE QUEEN OF SHEBA

WHEN the queen of Sheba heard of the fame of Solomon, she came to see him and to test him with hard questions. She arrived in Jerusalem with a very great train of attendants, with camels carrying spices, and much gold and precious stones. And when she had come to Solomon, she told him all the things that were on her mind. And Solomon answered all her questions, for there was nothing that he did not know.

And when the queen of Sheba had heard Solomon's wisdom, and seen the house that he had built, the food at his table, his servants, the magnificence of his ministers and his cupbearers and the entrance to the temple which he had built, there was no more spirit in her.

She said to the king: "What I heard in my own country about your wisdom and your deeds was all true. But I could not believe it until I had seen for myself. So I came, and behold, the half was not told me. Happy the men and happy the servants who stand continually before you and listen to your words of wisdom. Blessed be the Lord your God who favors you and has made you ruler over Israel. The Lord loved Israel forever, therefore he made you king to do judgment and justice."

She gave the king a hundred and twenty talents of gold, and great stores of spices and precious stones. Never before had there been so many spices as those which the queen of Sheba gave to king Solomon.

In exchange king Solomon gave the queen of Sheba everything that she desired and whatever she asked for. And so she went back to her own country, she and her servants.

Solomon grew very rich; he made a great throne of ivory and overlaid it with the best gold. All his drinking vessels were of gold and he had at sea a great navy which brought to his kingdom not only gold but silver and ivory and apes and peacocks. On land Solomon had an army of twelve thousand horsemen and one thousand four hundred chariots.

SOLOMON DIES AND THE KINGDOM IS DIVIDED

King Solomon exceeded all the kings of the earth for riches and wisdom and all the earth sought to hear the wisdom which God had put in his head. But in his riches and his splendor Solomon turned to evil ways. The Lord became angry with him for he burned incense and sacrificed unto other gods. The Lord made adversaries to rise up against him and among those who opposed him was Jeroboam, the son of one of his servants and a mighty man of valor.

And through a prophet, Ahijah the Shihonite, God spoke to Jeroboam saying:

"Because Solomon has not kept my ways and done what is right in my eyes, as did David his father, I will rend the kingdom out of his hands, and will give ten tribes to you. You shall be king over Israel but his son Rehoboam shall reign over one tribe in Jerusalem, the city where I have chosen to put my name."

And God did as he had promised. Solomon had reigned in Jerusalem over all Israel for forty years. He died and was buried in the city of David, his father. And Rehoboam reigned in Solomon's stead, but Israel under Jeroboam rose up against him. Jeroboam was made king over all Israel and reigned for twenty-two years. Rehoboam reigned seventeen years over Jerusalem and there was war between Rehoboam and Jeroboam all their days. And when each king died, he was succeeded by his son.

ELIJAH
A PROPHET
OF ISRAEL

The division in 922 B. C. of the united kingdom of Israel into two parts, the northern kingdom of Israel and the southern kingdom of Judah, was a momentous event in the history of the Hebrews. After about fifty years, a king named Ahab succeeded to the throne of Israel. He married Jezebel, daughter of the king of the Zidonians, and built an altar and a temple to the heathen god, Baal, in his capital city of Samaria. He was sternly rebuked for his evil ways and worship of Baal by the prophet, Elijah.

LIJAH the Tishbite, and inhabitant of Gilead, said to Ahab: "As the Lord God of Israel lives, before whom I stand, there will not be dew nor rain for years, unless I say the word."

Then the word of the Lord came to Elijah, saying: "Get away from here and turn eastward and hide yourself by the brook Cherith, which is this side of Jordan. There you shall drink of the brook, and I have commanded ravens to feed you there."

So he went and did as the Lord had commanded, and lived by the brook Cherith. And the ravens brought him bread and meat in the morning and again bread and meat in the evening, and he drank of the brook.

It came to pass, after a while, that the brook dried up, because there had been no rain in the land.

Then the word of the Lord came to him, saying: "Get up and go to Zarephath, which belongs to Zidon, and live there. You will find I have commanded a widow there to feed you."

402

ELIJAH HEALS
THE WIDOW'S SON

And when Elijah arrived at the gate of Zarephath he saw that the widow was there gathering sticks.

He called to her and said: "Fetch me, I beg of you, a little water in a vessel, so that I may have a drink." And as she was going to fetch it, he called to her and said: "Please bring me a morsel of bread."

She said: "As the Lord your God lives, I have not a loaf, but only a handful of meal in a barrel, and a little oil in a jar. As you see, I am gathering two sticks, that I may go in and prepare it for myself and my son, so that we may eat it and die."

Elijah said to her: "Do not fear. Go and do as you have said; but make me a little cake of it first, and bring it to me, and afterward make some for yourself and for your son. For the Lord God of Israel has said: 'The barrel of meal shall not be empty, nor the jar of oil fail, until the day when the Lord sends rain upon the earth.'"

She went and did as Elijah told her, and she and Elijah and her household ate for many days.

But it happened, after these things, that the son of the woman fell sick, and his sickness was so severe that there was no breath left in him.

The woman said to Elijah: "What have I done to you, O man of God? Have you come to me to remind me of my sins, and to kill my son?"

"Give me your son," he said to her, and he took him from her arms and carried him up to a loft where he stayed, and laid him upon his own bed.

Then he cried to the Lord and said: "O Lord my God, have you brought evil upon the widow with whom I am staying, by killing her son?"

Then he stretched himself out upon the child three times and cried to the Lord, and said: "O Lord my God, I beg you, let this child's soul come back to him."

The Lord heard the voice of Elijah, and the soul of the child came to him again, and he breathed. Then Elijah took the child and brought him down from the loft into the house, and gave him to his mother. And Elijah said: "See, your child lives!"

And the woman said to Elijah: "Now by this I know that you are a man of God, and that the word of the Lord which you preach is the truth."

ELIJAH AND THE PRIESTS OF BAAL

AND it came to pass after many days, that the word of the Lord came to Elijah in the third year of the famine, saying: "Go and show yourself to Ahab, and I will send rain upon the earth." And Elijah went to show himself to king Ahab.

When king Ahab saw Elijah, he said to him: "Are you the man who troubles Israel?"

Elijah answered: "It is not I who have troubled Israel, but you and your father's house, by forsaking the commandments of the Lord and following Baalim.

"Now send out and gather together all Israel at Mount Carmel, and the four hundred and fifty prophets of Baal, and the four hundred prophets of the groves who eat at queen Jezebel's table."

So Ahab sent word to all the children of Israel and gathered the prophets together at Mount Carmel.

Then Elijah came before all the people and said: "How long will you waver between two beliefs? If the Lord is God, follow him; if Baal, follow him."

The people answered not a word.

Then Elijah said to the people: "I, and I alone, remain a prophet of the Lord, but the prophets of Baal are four hundred and fifty men. Let them, then, get us two young bulls and let them choose one bull for themselves, and cut it in pieces and lay it on the wood, but put no fire under it. And I will dress the other bull and lay it on the wood and put no fire under it.

"Then you call on the name of your gods, and I will call on the name of the Lord, and the God that answers with fire, let him be God."

And all the people answered and said: "It is well spoken."

Elijah said to the prophets of Baal: "Choose one bull for yourselves and dress it first, for there are many of you. Call on the name of your gods, but do not put any fire under it."

They took the bull which was given them, and they dressed it and called on the name of Baal from morning until noon, saying: "O Baal, hear us." But there was no voice nor any answer, though they leaped upon the altar they had made.

At noon Elijah mocked them and said: "Cry aloud, for he is a god. Either he is talking, or he is busy, or he is on a journey, or perhaps he is asleep and must be awakened."

They cried aloud, and cut themselves, as was their custom, with knives and lances, until the blood gushed out upon their robes.

When midday was past, they worshiped before the altar until time for the evening sacrifice, and still there was neither a voice nor any answer nor any sign that their gods had heard them.

Then Elijah said to all the people: "Come near to me."

All the people gathered around him

Then he walked up to the altar of the Lord which had been broken down. Elijah took twelve stones, according to the number of the tribes of the sons of Jacob which made up Israel. With the stones he built an altar in the name of the Lord, and he made a trench round the altar, large enough to hold two measures of seed. He put the wood in order, and cut the young bull in pieces and laid it on the wood.

Then he said: "Fill four barrels with water and pour it on the burnt sacrifice and on the wood."

When they had done this, he said: "Do it a second time," and they did it a second time. And he said: "Do it a third time," and they did it a third time.

The water ran around the altar, and he filled the trench with water, too.

Then when it was time for the offering of the evening sacrifice, Elijah the prophet came near and said: "Lord God of Abraham, Isaac, and of Israel, let it be known today that you are the God in Israel, and that I am your servant and have done all these things at your command.

"Hear me, O Lord, hear me, that this people may know that you are the Lord God, and that you may have their hearts again."

Then the fire of the Lord came down and consumed the burnt sacrifice and the wood and the stones and the dust, and licked up the water that was in the trench.

When all the people saw it, they fell on their faces and said: "The Lord he is the God; the Lord he is the God."

And Elijah said to them: "Take the prophets of Baal; let not one of them escape."

And they took them; and Elijah brought them down to the brook Kishon and slew them there. And by evening the rains came and thus the famine was ended.

THE STILL
SMALL
VOICE

HAB recounted to Jezebel the story of all that Elijah had done, and how he had slain all the prophets of Baal.

So Jezebel sent a messenger to Elijah, saying: "Let the gods do to me and more still, if by this time tomorrow I do not take your life as you have taken theirs."

When Elijah heard this he arose and fled for his life, and went to Beersheba, where he left his servant. And he himself went a further day's journey into the wilderness and sat down under a juniper tree.

He prayed that he might die, and said: "It is enough, Lord. Take away my life, for I am no better than my fathers."

Then he lay down and slept under the tree and an angel awoke him, saying: "Arise and eat."

Elijah saw a cake and jar of water at his head, so he ate and drank, and slept again; and again the angel awakened him to eat. And fortified by the food, he traveled forty days and nights until he arrived at Mount Horeb.

He lived there in a cave and the word of the Lord came to him, asking: "What are you doing here, Elijah?"

Elijah said: "I have cared greatly for the Lord God of hosts, but the children of Israel have forsaken your covenants, thrown down your altars and slain your prophets with the sword. Only I remain, and they are seeking to kill me."

God said: "Go forth, and stand upon the mountain."

He did so, and a great wind blew upon the mountain and smashed the rocks, but the Lord was not in the wind. After the wind came an earth-

quake, but the Lord was not in the earthquake; and after the earthquake a fire, but the Lord was not in the fire; and after the fire, a still small voice.

When Elijah heard the voice, he wrapped his face in his mantle and stood in the opening of the cave.

And the voice said: "What are you doing here, Elijah?"

And Elijah said: "I have cared greatly for the Lord God of hosts, but the children of Israel have forsaken your covenant, and thrown down your altars and slain your prophets with the sword. Only I remain, and they are seeking to kill me."

The Lord said to him: "Go to Damascus and anoint Hazael to be king over Syria; and anoint Jehu, son of Nimshi, to be king over Israel; and Elisha, the son of Shaphat, shall you anoint to be prophet after you."

So Elijah departed and found Elisha whom the Lord had named working at the plough. And Elisha arose and went after Elijah and became his servant.

NABOTH'S VINEYARD

NABOTH the Jezreelite had a vineyard which was situated close to the palace of Ahab, the king of Samaria.

Ahab said to Naboth: "Give me your vineyard, that I may turn it into a herb garden, for it is so near my house. In exchange I will give you a better vineyard, or if you prefer, I will give you its value in money."

Naboth answered: "The Lord forbid that I should give you the land which I have inherited from my forefathers."

Ahab went back to his house, depressed and vexed because of what Naboth had said. He lay down on his bed and turned his face to the wall and refused to eat.

Jezebel, his wife, came in and said: "Why are you so sad that you refuse to eat?"

Ahab said: "Because I asked Naboth to let me have his vineyard, and I offered to pay for it or give him another vineyard in exchange, but he would have none of it."

Jezebel said: "Are you not king of Israel? Get up, eat and be merry, and I shall see to it that you get Naboth's vineyard."

She wrote letters in Ahab's name and sealed them with his seal, and sent them to the elders and the nobles who lived in the same city as Naboth. In the letters she wrote: "Proclaim a fast and set Naboth on high among the people, and set two men, sons of Belial, before him, to testify against him and say that he has blasphemed against God and the king. Then take him out of the city and stone him until he dies."

The elders and nobles of the city did as Jezebel had instructed them. They proclaimed a fast, accused Naboth of blasphemy, and stoned him to death. Then they sent a message to Jezebel, saying: "Naboth is stoned and dead."

When Jezebel heard this, she said to Ahab: "Go and take possession of Naboth's vineyard which he refused to sell to you, for he is no longer alive."

So Ahab went down and took possession of the vineyard of Naboth the Jezreelite.

But the word of the Lord came to Elijah the Tishbite, and he went down to see Ahab, who was in the vineyard which he had taken from Naboth.

And as Elijah came, Ahab said: "Have you found me, O my enemy?"

Elijah said: "I have found you,

because you have sold yourself to work evil in the eyes of the Lord. The Lord will bring evil upon you and destroy your posterity, and the dogs shall eat Jezebel by the wall of Jezreel."

When Ahab heard these words he rent his clothes and fasted and went humbly in sackcloth and ashes. Because of his humility God told Elijah: "I will not bring the evil in his days; but in his son's days I will bring the evil upon his house."

THE PARTING OF ELIJAH AND ELISHA

ND it came to pass that when the Lord decided to take Elijah up into heaven in a whirlwind, Elijah was with Elisha, his faithful follower, in Gilgal. Setting out from Gilgal together, Elijah and Elisha went to Bethel and Jericho.

And the followers of the prophets who were at Jericho came to Elisha and said to him: "Do you know that the Lord is going to take away your master from you today?"

He said: "Yes, I know it. Hold your peace."

And Elijah said to him: "Wait here, I beg you, for the Lord has told me to go to Jordan."

But Elisha said to him: "As the Lord lives, and as your soul lives, I will not leave you."

So the two went on. And fifty of the followers of the prophets went and stood at a distance to watch. Elijah and Elisha stood beside the Jordan.

Elijah took his mantle and folded it over, and struck the waters so that they were divided on either side, and the two men went across on dry ground.

It happened, when they had crossed over, that Elijah said to Elisha: "Ask what you will of me, before I am taken away from you."

Elisha said: "Let a double portion of your spirit be upon me, I beg of you."

"You have asked a hard thing," Elijah said. "Nevertheless, if you see me when I am taken from you, you shall have your wish; but if not, you shall not have it."

It happened, as they went on and talked together, that a chariot of fire and horses of fire appeared, and swept them apart; and Elijah went up by a whirlwind into heaven.

Elisha saw it, and he cried: "My father, my father! The chariot of Israel and its horsemen!" Then he could not see Elijah any more, and he took hold of his own robe and ripped it in two.

He picked up Elijah's mantle, which had fallen from him, and went back and stood by the bank of the Jordan. He took Elijah's mantle and struck the waters and said: "Where is the Lord God of Elijah?" And when he had struck the waters, they parted on either side of him and Elisha crossed over.

When the followers of the prophets who had come to watch saw him, they said: "The spirit of Elijah rests on Elisha."

And they came to meet him, and bowed themselves to the ground before him.

And the men of Jericho said to him: "You can see that the situation of the city is pleasant, but the water is bad and the ground barren."

Elisha said: "Bring me a new jar and put salt in it."

They did so and he went to the source of the water and threw in the salt and said: "The Lord says that these waters are healed and they will cause no more death or barren lands." So the waters were healed for ever according to the word of Elisha.

ELISHA HEALS A LEPER

Naaman, captain of the army of the king of Syria, was a great man among his master's followers, and honorable. Through him, the Lord had granted freedom to Syria. He was a man of great courage; but he was a leper.

The Syrians had gone out by companies and had brought back as a captive out of the land of Israel a little girl. She was a maidservant to Naaman's wife.

She said to her mistress: "I would to God my lord were with the prophet who is in Samaria, for he would cure him of his leprosy."

When the king of Syria heard what the girl had spoken, he said: "Go now, go, and I will send a letter to the king of Israel."

Naaman departed with the letter, and took with him ten talents of silver, and

six thousand pieces of gold, and ten complete changes of clothing.

He delivered to the king of Israel the letter, which said: "When you receive this letter, you will see that I have sent to you with it Naaman, my servant, that you may cure him of his leprosy."

When the king of Israel had read the letter, he tore his clothes and said: "Am I God, to kill and to make alive, that this man sends a man to me to be cured of his leprosy? Take heed, for he seeks to pick a quarrel with me."

Now when Elisha, the man of God, heard that the king of Israel was troubled, he sent word to the king, saying: "Why did you tear your clothes? Let the man come to me, and he shall know that there is a prophet in Israel."

So Naaman came with his horses and his chariot, and stood at the door of the house of Elisha.

Elisha sent a messenger to him, saying: "Go and wash in the Jordan seven times, and your flesh will be healed again, and you will be well."

But Naaman was angry and turned away, saying: "I had thought, 'He will surely come out to me and stand there and call on the name of the Lord his God and strike his hand on the place and cure the leprosy.' Are not Abana and Pharpar, the rivers of Damascus, better than all the waters of Israel? May I not wash in them and be cured?"

His servants spoke to him, and said: "My father, if the prophet Elisha had ordered you to do some difficult thing, would you not have done it? How much better to obey when he says to you, 'Wash and be made well.' "

Then Naaman went and dipped himself seven times in the Jordan, just as the man of God had said, and his flesh was once again like the flesh of a little child, and he was well.

He went back to the man of God, he and all his company, and came and stood before him, and he said: "Now

I know that there is no God in all the earth but in Israel. And so I beg of you to accept a token of your servant's gratitude."

But Elisha said: "As the Lord lives, I will accept nothing. Go in peace."

And Naaman went on his way.

ELISHA'S SERVANT FOLLOWS NAAMAN

But Gehazi, the servant of Elisha, said to himself: "See, my master has refused to accept the gift offered by this Naaman the Syrian. As the Lord lives, I will run after him and obtain something for myself."

So Gehazi followed Naaman, and when Naaman saw him running after him, he came down from his chariot and went to meet him, and said: "Is all well?"

Gehazi said: "All is well. My master has sent me to tell you that two young men of the sons of the prophets have just now arrived from Mount Ephraim, and will you give them a talent of silver and two changes of garments?"

Naaman said: "Be content, take two talents." And he packed two talents of silver and the changes of clothing in two bags and gave them to two of his servants, and they carried them for Gehazi.

When he came to the tower, Gehazi took the bags from them and put them in the house, and told the men to go. Then he went and stood before his master.

And Elisha said to him: "Where have you been, Gehazi?"

He said: "Your servant has not been anywhere."

Elisha said: "Did I not go in spirit with you when the man left his chariot to meet you? Is this the moment to receive money, and to receive garments and olive groves, and vineyards and sheep and oxen and menservants and maidservants? The leprosy of which Naaman was cured has passed over to you and to your descendants for ever more."

And Gehazi went from his presence a leper as white as snow.

THE ANOINTING OF JEHU

The curing of Naaman took place during one of the brief truces between Israel and Syria, which more often than not were fighting against each other. In one battle, Ahab, king of Israel, was killed. He was soon followed to the throne of Israel by Joram, a son. Meanwhile, in the south, Ahaziah, a grandson of Ahab, became king of Judah upon the death of his father, who had married a daughter of Ahab. Jezebel, Ahab's wife, remained in Israel. Such was the situation when Elisha set about helping to fulfill the prophecy of Elijah concerning destruction of the "posterity of Ahab."

ELISHA the prophet called one of his followers and said to him: "Go to Ramoth-Gilead and look for Jehu, the son of Jehoshaphat, the son of Nimshi, and cause him to leave his friends and take him into an inner room. Then take this vial of oil and pour it on his head and say: 'Thus says the Lord, I have anointed you king over Israel.' Then open the door and flee."

So the young man, who was himself a prophet, went to Ramoth-Gilead and told Jehu that he had a message for him. Jehu arose and went into his house, and the prophet poured oil on to his head and said: "Thus says the Lord God of Israel, I have anointed you king over the people of the Lord, even over Israel. And you shall smite the house of Ahab your master, that I may avenge the blood of my servants the prophets, and the blood of all the servants of the Lord, at the hand of Jezebel."

Then the young man opened the door and fled. Jehu went back to his people and one of them said to him:

"Is all well? What did this madman want with you?"

Jehu told them what the young man had said and they blew on trumpets and said: "Jehu is king." So Jehu rode in a chariot towards Jezreel, where king Joram of Israel, son of Ahab, was lying

wounded after a battle with king Hazael of Syria.

A watchman stood on the tower in Jezreel and he saw the company of Jehu approaching and told the king of it. Joram said: "Send a horseman to meet them and ask: 'Do you come in peace?'"

So the horseman went to meet Jehu and said: "The king asks if you come in peace?" Jehu said: "What have you to do with peace? Get behind me."

As he did not return, the watchman sent out another messenger who asked Jehu the same question, and again Jehu answered: "What have you to do with peace? Get behind me."

Then the watchman said: "The messenger reached them, but he has not returned; and the driving is like the driving of Jehu, for he drives furiously."

JEHU SLAYS JORAM

Joram said: "Make ready." His chariot was prepared, and together with Ahaziah, king of Judah, king Joram of Israel went forth to battle, and met Jehu in the land that had belonged to Naboth the Jezreelite. And Jehu drew a bow with all his might and smote Joram between his arms and the arrow went out at his heart, and he sank down in his chariot.

Then Jehu said to Bidkar, his captain: "Take him up and throw him into the field of Naboth the Jezreelite, for today the blood of Naboth and his sons has been avenged on his own ground."

When Ahaziah saw what had happened, he fled by way of a garden house, but Jehu followed and smote him; and he fled to Megiddo and died there. Thus Jehu overcame both Joram of Israel and Ahaziah of Judah.

JEZEBEL IS KILLED

When Jehu came to Jezreel, Jezebel heard about it. She painted her face and dressed her hair and looked down from a window. As Jehu entered through the city gate, she said: "Was there any peace for Zimri who killed his master?"

He looked up to the window and said: "Who is on my side?"

Two or three servants looked down at him, and he said: "Throw her down." So they threw her down, and he trod her underfoot.

When Jehu had come in, he ate and drank, and said: "Go, see now this accursed woman and bury her; for she is a king's daughter."

And thus was fulfilled the prophecy of Elijah the Tishbite concerning queen Jezebel.

THE CROWNING OF JOASH

Jehu completed his destruction of the family of Ahab by slaying seventy of his sons. After this he had all Israel's Baal worshipers put to death. Jehu's slaying of a grandson of Ahab, king Ahaziah of Judah, was to set in motion further killings by Ahaziah's widowed mother, Athaliah, who was eager to be queen of Judah.

HEN Athaliah of Judah saw that her son Ahaziah was dead, she caused all the royal children to be put to death.

But Jehosheba, the wife of Jehoiada, the high priest, rescued Joash, the son of Ahaziah, by hiding him and his nurse in the sleeping apartment, so that he was not slain. The boy was concealed for six years in the house of the Lord with Jehosheba and Jehoiada, while queen Athaliah reigned in Judah.

In the seventh year Jehoiada fetched all the rulers and the chief captains, and brought them to the house of the Lord, and made a covenant with them.

They swore a solemn oath to him, and he brought them the king's son saying: "This is the thing you shall do. A third of your number shall come into the house of the Lord on the sabbath and keep watch over the king's house. A third shall be at the gate of Sur; and a third at the gate behind the guard, so that the house of the Lord will be safely guarded. The two companies who go off duty on the sabbath will also join in keeping the watch of the house of the Lord. You shall guard the king by surrounding him each man with his sword in hand. If anyone comes within the precincts, he shall be killed. You shall remain with the king both when he goes out and when he comes in."

The captains did as they were commanded, and Jehoiada gave them king David's spears and shields, which were in the temple. The guards stood fully armed throughout the temple, surrounding the king, and Jehoiada presented the young Joash to them and crowned him. They gave him the royal insignia and anointed him, and all the people clapped their hands and said: "God save the king."

When Athaliah heard the noise of the guard and the people, she came to the temple of the Lord. She looked in and saw the king standing by a pillar, as was the custom at a coronation, and the princes and the trumpeters beside him, and all the people rejoicing to the sound of trumpets.

Athaliah rent her clothes and cried: "Treason! Treason!"

Jehoiada said to the captains of the host: "Take her out of the temple and if anybody follows her, put him to death with the sword. She must not die within the precincts of the house of the Lord."

So they seized her and took her on to the road by which horses approached the palace. There she was slain.

Jehoiada made a covenant between the Lord and the king and the people, that they should all be the Lord's people. And the people of the land went into the house of Baal and broke it down. They smashed its altars and its images and they slew Mattan, the priest of Baal, before the altar.

Joash came by way of the guards' gate from the house of the Lord to the king's house, and there he reigned under the name Jehoash.

THE DEATH
OF
ELISHA

OW Elisha had fallen ill and was on his deathbed. And king Jehoash of Israel, a grandson of Jehu, came to Elisha and wept over him and said: "O my father, my father, the chariot of Israel and the horsemen thereof."

Elisha said to him: "Take a bow and arrows." And he took a bow and arrows.

Elisha said to the King of Israel: "Put your hand on the bow." He did so, and Elisha put his hands upon the king's hands. He said: "Open the window to the east." The king opened it.

Then Elisha said: "Shoot," and the king shot.

"The arrow of the Lord's deliverance," said Elisha, "and the arrow of deliverance from Syria. You shall smite the Syrians in Aphek till you have consumed them. Now, take the arrows." The king took them.

Elisha said: "Strike the ground."

He struck it three times and then did so no more.

The man of God was angry with him and said: "You should have struck five or six times, for then you would have struck Syria until you had destroyed it, whereas now you will strike Syria three times only."

And Elisha died and was buried.

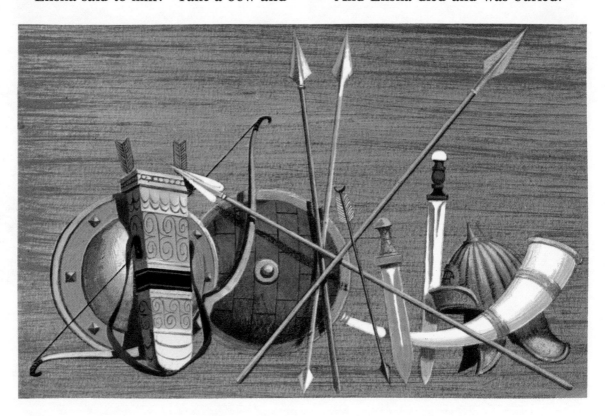

from the BOOKS OF AMOS, HOSEA, and ISAIAH

WARNINGS FROM THE PROPHETS

Woe to them that are at ease in Zion,
and cause the violence to come near;
That lie upon beds of ivory,
and stretch themselves upon their couches,
And eat the lambs out of the flock,
and the calves from the midst of the stall,
That chant to the sound of the viol,
and invent for themselves
instruments of music, like David;
That drink wine in bowls,
and anoint themselves with ointments!
Shall not the land tremble for this,
and every one mourn that dwells therein?
And it shall come to pass in that day,
says the Lord God, that I will cause
the sun to go down at noon,
And I will turn your feast into mourning,
and all your songs into lamentation.
Behold the days come, says the Lord,
that I will send a famine in the land;
Not a famine of bread,
nor a thirst for water,
but of hearing the words of the Lord.
And they shall wander from sea to sea,
and from the north even to the east,
They shall run to and fro
to seek the word of the Lord,
and shall not find it.

In accordance with Elisha's dying words, Israel won three battles against Syrian forces. But after the prosperous reign of Jeroboam II, son of Jehoash, Israel became weaker and weaker, caught up in a series of internal political intrigues and assassinations.

This beginning of Israel's end was predicted with scorn and vehemence by a visionary shepherd from Judah. This was Amos, the first of many prophets to forecast the downfall of the Hebrew nations. He preached in Israel during the end of Jeroboam's rule around the middle of the eighth century B. C. In particular he attacked the life of luxury and spiritual indifference that he saw as the source of Israel's weakness.

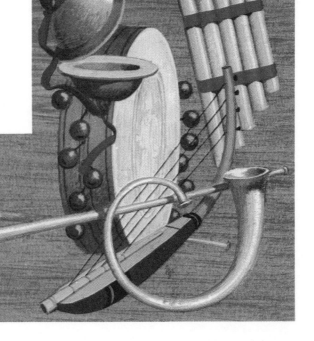

HOSEA'S MESSAGE OF HOPE

Amos was followed closely, in time and in theme, by the prophet Hosea. He preached also in the northern kingdom of Israel, as the dark shadow of a power far more dangerous than Syria stretched closer and closer to Israel's borders. While predicting the approaching disaster, Hosea also held out hope, calling for repentance and promising redemption through God's mercy and love.

O Israel, return unto the Lord your God,
   for you have fallen by your iniquity.
Take with you words,
   and turn to the Lord.
Say unto him, Take away all iniquity,
   and receive us graciously.
His branches shall spread,
   and his beauty shall be as the olive tree.
They that dwell in his shadow shall return;
   they shall revive as the corn
   and grow as the vine.
Who is wise, and he shall understand
   these things;
   prudent, and shall know them?
For the ways of the Lord are right,
   and the just shall walk in them;
But the transgressors shall fall therein.

ISAIAH'S VISION

Both during and after the time of Hosea in Israel, one of the greatest of all Hebrew prophets, Isaiah, was active in Judah, the southern kingdom. Like Israel, Judah had enjoyed a long period of peace and prosperity—during much of the reigns of Jehoash's son, Amaziah, and grandson, Uzziah.

Isaiah was not only a visionary preacher but also a wise statesman and adviser of Judah's kings through years of constant crises. These arose from military threats from without, from traditional opponents such as Syria and Israel, and from a new and dangerous friend, Assyria.

In the year that king Uzziah died, I saw the Lord sitting on a throne lifted up on high, and his train filled the temple. Above it stood the seraphim. Each had six wings: with two he covered his face, with two he covered his feet, and with two he did fly.

One cried to another and said: "Holy, holy, holy is the Lord of hosts. The whole earth is full of his glory."

The posts of the door moved at the voice of him who cried, and the house was filled with smoke. Then I said:

"Woe is me! For I am ruined, because I am a man of unclean lips and I dwell in the midst of people of unclean lips, and now my eyes have seen the king, the Lord of hosts."

Then one of the seraphim flew at me, bearing in his hand a live coal which he had taken from the altar with tongs. He laid it upon my mouth and said:

"Behold, this has touched your lips; your wickedness is taken away, and your sin is removed."

And I heard the voice of the Lord saying: "Whom shall I send? Who will go for us?"

"Here I am," I said. "Send me."

And the Lord said:

"Go and tell this people: 'You hear, but you do not understand. You see, but you do not know what you see.'

"Weigh down the heart of this people and make their ears heavy, and shut their eyes, lest they see with their eyes, and hear with their ears and understand with their hearts, and change their ways and become healed."

Then I said, "How long, O Lord?" And God answered:

"Until the cities are wasted and without inhabitants, and the houses are vacant, and the land is utterly desolate. Then the Lord will have removed the men far away, and the whole land will be forsaken."

RESPITE
FOR
JERUSALEM

"Behold, a maiden shall conceive,
  and bear a son,
And shall call his name Immanuel,
Butter and honey shall he eat,
That he may know to refuse the evil,
  and choose the good.
For before the child shall know to refuse
  the evil, and choose the good,
The land that you despise shall be
  forsaken of both her kings.
The people that walked in darkness
Have seen a great light;

ZZIAH ruled fifty-two years in Jerusalem and when he died Jotham, his son, ruled in his place. When Jotham died, they buried him in the city of David, and Ahaz, his son, ruled in his place.

Now it came to pass in the days of Ahaz that the king of Syria and the king of Israel attacked Jerusalem, but could not conquer it. And God said to Isaiah, "Go forth and meet Ahaz and say to him:

" 'Take heed and be quiet. Fear not these two smoking firebrands, Syria and Israel. For, although they have made an evil plan against you, it shall not come to pass.' "

Moreover, God spoke to Ahaz, saying:

"Ask for a sign of the Lord your God."

"I will not ask," Ahaz said. "I will not test the Lord."

Then Isaiah said:

"Hear now, O House of David. It is a small thing for you to weary men, but will you weary my God also? The Lord himself shall give you a sign:

Upon those that dwell in the land
  of shadow of death
The light has shined.
For unto us a child is born,
  unto us a son is given:
And the government shall be upon his
  shoulder:
And his name shall be called Wonderful,
  Counselor, the Mighty God,
The Everlasting Father,
  the Prince of Peace.
Of the spread of his kingdom and his peace
  there shall be no end,
  from now on, even forever.
The zeal of the Lord of hosts will perform
  this."

Ahaz sent messengers to the king of Assyria, saying:

"Come and save me from the king of Syria and the king of Israel, which rise up against me."

And Ahaz took the silver and the gold that was found in the house of the Lord and in the king's treasury, and sent it as a present to the king of Assyria. Then the king of Assyria answered Ahaz's plea and went out against Damascus and killed the king of Syria.

The Assyrians not only overthrew Damascus and the king of Syria; they also a few years later besieged and captured Samaria, capital of the northern kingdom. The downfall of Samaria in 722 B. C. meant the end of Israel as a nation. The Israelites were marched off and scattered through other parts of the Assyrian Empire.

Meanwhile Judah the southern kingdom managed miraculously to survive. The Assyrians attacked Jerusalem in 701 B. C. but their troops were struck by plague and forced to withdraw. The aged Isaiah saw in these events the deliverance of his people through the working of the hand of God. This was an important function of the prophets: to interpret and demonstrate the actions of God in history.

from the
BOOKS OF II KINGS
and JEREMIAH

JOSIAH
A RIGHTEOUS
KING

After king Ahaz's death, his son Heze-kiah reigned, followed by Manasseh, Amon and then Josiah. It was during Josiah's rule, in the last quarter of the seventh century B. C., that one of the major events in Hebrew history occurred, the finding of the Book of the Law, Deuteronomy. This document, which contains many of the rules for behavior and worship followed by Hebrews and Christians to this day, deeply impressed king Josiah. He tried to put its com-mands into effect by abolishing many of the pagan elements that had crept into the worship of his people.

OSIAH was eight years old when he began to rule, and he ruled thirty-one years in Jerusalem. He did that which was right in the sight of the Lord and followed in the steps of David his fore-father, and turned not aside to the right nor to the left.

And it came to pass in the eighteenth year of king Josiah's reign that the king sent Shaphan the son of Azaliah, the scribe, to the house of the Lord.

And when Shaphan the scribe went to the temple of the Lord, Hilkiah the high priest said to him:

"I have found the Book of the Law in the house of the Lord." And Hilkiah gave the book to Shaphan, and he read it.

Then Shaphan the scribe showed the king the book, saying:

"Hilkiah the priest has delivered this book to me."

And Shaphan read it before the king.

And when the king had heard the words of the Book of the Law he

read into their ears all the words of the book of the covenant which was found in the house of the Lord.

The king stood by a pillar and made a covenant before the Lord, to walk in his ways and to keep his commandments and follow his words and his laws, with all his heart and with all his soul, and to live up to the words of this covenant that were written in the book; and all the people agreed to the covenant.

JOSIAH BANISHES IDOL WORSHIP

Then the king commanded Hilkiah the high priest, and the priests of the second order, and the keepers of the door, to bring forth out of the temple of the Lord all the vessels that were made for Baal and his sacred wood, and for all the other gods; and he burned them outside of Jerusalem in the fields of Kidron, and carried the ashes of them to Bethel.

He put down the idolatrous priests, whom the kings of Judah had ordained to burn incense in the high places in the cities of Judah and in the places round about Jerusalem, and also those who burned incense to Baal, to the sun, and to the moon, and to the planets, and to all the various gods. Josiah destroyed also the workers with ghosts and magic, and the wizards, and the images, and the idols and all the evil things that were to be found in the land of Judah and in Jerusalem, so that he might live up to the words of the law which were written in the book that Hilkiah the priest found in the house of the Lord.

There had been no king like Josiah. For he turned to the Lord with all his heart, and with all his soul, and with all his might, according to all the law of Moses; neither did any come after him who was his equal.

tore his clothes, for he knew his fathers had not listened to the words of this book, to obey all the laws that were written down for them.

The king sent for all the elders of Judah and of Jerusalem. Then he went up to the house of the Lord, taking all the men of Judah and all the inhabitants of Jerusalem with him, both the priests and the prophets and all the people, both small and great, and he

THE FALL
OF
JERUSALEM

your herds. They shall eat up your vines and your fig trees. And it shall come to pass when you shall say, 'Why does the Lord our God do these things to us?' that I shall answer, 'You have forsaken me and served strange gods in your land. Therefore shall you serve strangers in a land that is not yours.'

"Hear now this, O foolish people, which have eyes and see not, which have ears and hear not."

During king Josiah's reign, another great Hebrew figure appeared as a prophet in Judah. This was Jeremiah, who like Isaiah was both an inspired spokesman for his God and a shrewd analyst of current affairs. Active under five kings of Judah during a time when his country was always at the mercy of stronger powers, Jeremiah often advised compliance. This frequently put him at odds with Judah's leaders.

In the last years of Josiah's rule, Nineveh, the Assyrian capital, fell to the forces of Babylon. Jeremiah saw the rise of this power in the east as an evil omen for Jerusalem and the kingdom of Judah.

HE words of the Lord came to the prophet Jeremiah, saying:

"I will bring a nation upon you from far away, O house of Israel. It is a mighty nation. It is an ancient nation, a nation whose language you do not know, nor understand. And they shall eat up your harvest and your bread, which your sons and daughters should eat. They shall eat up your flocks and

JUDAH IS CONTROLLED
BY FOREIGN POWERS

King Josiah was slain in battle at Megiddo, and his son Jehohoaz reigned in his place. But after three months he was deposed by Pharaoh, king of Egypt, who then made his brother, Jehoiakim, king.

Now Pharaoh demanded tribute of

one thousand talents of silver and one talent of gold from the land of Judah, so Jehoiakim taxed the people to find the silver and gold to give to Pharaoh. He was twenty-five years old when he began to rule, and he did that which was evil in the sight of the Lord.

During his reign, Nebuchadnezzar, king of Babylon, came to Jerusalem, and Jehoiakim became his vassal. After three years he rebelled against him.

But the Lord sent bands of Chaldees

his territory between the Nile and the Euphrates.

Jehoiachin ruled for only three months. Then Nebuchadnezzar, king of Babylon, came up to besiege Jerusalem, and Jehoiachin surrendered himself to Nebuchadnezzar with his mother and his servants, his princes and his officers. The king of Babylon took him prisoner and he also took away all the treasures of the house of the Lord and the treasures of the king's

and Syrians and Moabites and bands of the children of Ammon against Judah, as a punishment for former sins. Jehoiakim fought in vain against them until his death, when Jehoiachin, his son, ruled in his place.

By now the king of Egypt had lost his power and remained behind his own frontiers, for the king of Babylon had taken possession of all

house. And he cut in pieces all the vessels of gold which Solomon had made for the temple of the Lord.

He carried away all the princes, seven thousand mighty men of valor, a thousand craftsmen and blacksmiths —in all ten thousand captives. Only the poorest people were left in the country.

Nebuchadnezzar took Jehoiachin

away to Babylon, and Jehoiachin's mother and his wives and his officers, and all that were strong and likely warriors. All were taken to Babylon.

And the king of Babylon made Mattaniah, uncle of Jehoiachin, king of Judah in his place. And he changed Mattaniah's name to Zedekiah.

Zedekiah was twenty-one years old when he began to rule and he ruled eleven years in Jerusalem. And he did that which was evil in the sight of the Lord, according to all that done by Jehoiakim.

And it came to pass that Zedekiah rebelled against the king of Babylon. So in the ninth year of his reign in the tenth month, in the tenth day of the month, Nebuchadnezzar, king of Babylon, came with all his army and laid siege against Jerusalem.

JEREMIAH FORETELLS THE FATE OF ZEDEKIAH

Then Zedekiah the king sent two priests to Jeremiah the prophet, saying:

"Pray to the Lord our God for us."

At that time, Jeremiah was not in prison, as he often was, but was going about freely among the people. Pharaoh's army had set out from Egypt, and when the Chaldeans heard of this, they departed from their siege of Jerusalem.

The word of the Lord came to Jeremiah, saying:

"This you shall say to the king of Judah: 'Behold, Pharaoh's army which has set out to help you, shall go back to Egypt, and the Chaldeans shall come again and attack this city and burn it down. Do not deceive yourselves, says the Lord, or tell yourselves that the Chaldeans shall go away again, for they shall not depart.

" 'Even if you were to defeat the whole Chaldean army, and there were none left but wounded men, still would

each one of them rise in his tent, and burn this city with fire.' "

But some of the nobles, hearing what Jeremiah had told the king, that the city was going to fall into the hands of Babylon, went to the king and said:

"We entreat you to allow us to put this man to death, for by his words he is sapping the fighting spirit of the people."

"He is in your power," Zedekiah said. "The king can do nothing against your will."

So they took Jeremiah and threw him into the dungeon of Machiah the son of Hammelech, which was a cistern in the court of the prison. They let Jeremiah down with cords into the underground dungeon. There was no water in it, only mud. And Jeremiah sank in the mud.

Now Ebed-melech the Ethiopian, who was one of the king's slaves, heard what had happened to Jeremiah, and he spoke to the king who was sitting in judgment at the gate of Benjamin. He said:

"My Lord King, these men have done wrong in casting Jeremiah the prophet into the dungeon. He will die from hunger there, for there is no more bread in the city."

So the king told Ebed-melech the Ethiopian to take thirty men and rescue Jeremiah from the dungeon before he starved to death.

Ebed-melech took the men and collected some old rags and scraps of material and set them down by ropes into the dungeon. Then he called Jeremiah, saying:

"Put these rags under your armpits to protect you from the rope."

Jeremiah did so, and they pulled him up out of the muddy cistern, and he was sent back into a better prison. King Zedekiah sent for him again, and bade him come to the entrance of the temple.

"One thing I will ask you," said the king. "Hide nothing from me."

"But if I tell you the truth," said Jeremiah, "will you not have me put to death? And if I give you advice, will you not disregard it?"

Then king Zedekiah swore a secret oath to Jeremiah, and said:

"As the Lord our Creator lives, I will not have you put to death, nor will I hand you over to the men who want to kill you."

ZEDEKIAH IGNORES JEREMIAH'S ADVICE

Jeremiah the prophet answered king Zedekiah and said:

"Thus says the Lord, the God of hosts, the God of Israel: If you will go forth to the officers of the king of Babylon, your life will be spared. This city will not be destroyed by fire, and you and your family will survive. But if you will not go forth to the king of Babylon's officers, then this city will be given into the power of the Chaldeans, and they will burn it to the ground, and you will not escape out of their hand."

"I am afraid of the Jews who have gone over to Babylon," said king Zedekiah. "If I surrender, the Chaldeans may hand me over to them, and they will ill-treat me."

"They will not hand you over to the Jews," Jeremiah said. "I beg of you to obey the voice of the Lord, for then all will go well with you, and your life will be spared. If you do not, all your wives and children will be taken by the Babylonians, and because of you the city will be burned with fire."

And king Zedekiah said to Jeremiah:

"Tell no man about this talk of ours and you shall not die. If the nobles hear that I have been talking with you and question you with threats, tell them that you came to plead with me not to be sent back in the dungeon.

The nobles did come and did ask Jeremiah what he and the king had said, and Jeremiah answered as the king had told him. So nobody knew what had been said between them, and nothing more was done about it.

Jeremiah remained in the prison until the day that Jerusalem fell. He was there when Jerusalem was taken.

JERUSALEM IS DESTROYED

HE Chaldeans laid siege to Jerusalem during eleven years of Zedekiah's reign. And on the ninth day of the fourth month of the siege, the famine spread over the city, and there was no bread for the people in the land.

The city was overcome, and the men of the army fled by night, by way of a gate between two walls, which was near the king's garden, for the Chaldeans were all around the city. And the king went off towards the plain. The army of the Chaldeans pursued the king and overtook him on the plains of Jericho, and all his army was scattered.

So they took the king and brought him up to the king of Babylon at Riblah, and they passed judgment upon him.

They slew the sons of Zedekiah before his eyes, and put out the eyes of Zedekiah, and bound him with fetters of brass, and carried him to Babylon.

A LAMENT FOR JERUSALEM

How lonely sits the city
    that once was full of people!
How like a widow she has become
    that was great among the nations,
    and a princess among the provinces.
Now she is a vassal.
She weeps sadly at night, and her tears
    are on her cheeks.
Among all her lovers she has none to
    comfort her.
All her friends have dealt treacherously
    with her.
They have become her enemies.
In the days of her affliction
    and her miseries
Jerusalem remembered all the pleasant
    things which she had in the days of old.
When her people fell into the hands
    of the enemy, nobody helped her.
Jerusalem has grievously sinned, therefore
    she is removed.
All that honored her despise her.
Is it nothing to you, all ye that pass by?
Behold and see if there be any sorrow
    like the sorrow which has been done to me,
With which the Lord has afflicted me
    in the day of his fierce anger.

441

ILLUSTRATED
GLOSSARY

"As the sand that is on the seashore" (p. 396)

This phrase means that King Solomon had as much wisdom and understanding as there is sand on the seashore.

Assyria (p. 426)

Assyria was a country located on the Tigris River in northern Mesopotamia, encompassing much of what is modern-day Iraq. Its Semitic inhabitants were a people of great cruelty. They had a strong and efficient army, and in the 9th century B.C. they began to invade neighboring countries. Israel's King Ahab helped to defeat them.

For a century, the Assyrians made no more trouble for the Hebrews. Then in 735 B.C. they again moved against the Northern Kingdom and conquered it. Assyria won other wars and was able to build an empire from Egypt to beyond the Tigris.

Babylon (p. 434)

Babylon was the capital of the Babylonian Empire and was one of the most important and beautiful cities of its time. The Babylonians conquered the Assyrian Empire, which included the Northern Kingdom of Israel, during the end of the 7th century B.C. In 597 B.C., they conquered the Southern Kingdom.

"Blasphemed against God" (p. 410)

A person who speaks God's name without respect commits blasphemy. The Hebrews considered blasphemy so serious an offense that the blasphemer could be stoned to death.

Camels (p. 400)

The camel used in biblical lands was a one-humped animal now called the

dromedary. Camels make excellent beasts of burden in the desert. They are able to go for days without drinking because their stomachs can store water and they sweat little. Camels will eat desert plants such as thorns and thistles and their humps are made of stored fat which allows them to go without food for days.

Chaldeans (p. 436)

The Chaldeans were the inhabitants of Babylon. They were powerful fighters who were greatly feared by their neighbors.

Cistern (p. 436)

Rainwater was stored in large man-made wells called cisterns, which were usually cut from rock and lined with stones. Some homes had their own cisterns since every drop of water was prized in those dry Bible lands. The water in cisterns often became dirty and people preferred drinking water from wells or springs, and using cistern water for other purposes.

City of David (p. 428)

After King David conquered the fortress of Zion he built a city there, which was named Jerusalem. It was often called the City of David.

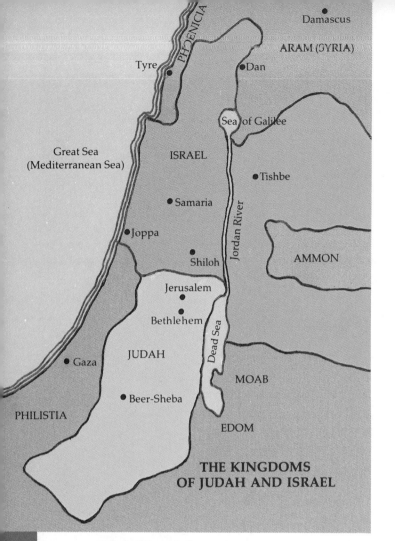

After King Solomon's reign, Israel was divided into two kingdoms, Israel and Judah.

Jezreelite (p. 410)

Naboth was a Jezreelite from the town of Jezreel, located on the Plain of Jezreel. Some of the best farmland in the Northern Kingdom was located there. The soil was excellent for growing fruit and grain.

Leper (p. 414)

A leper is someone who suffers from leprosy (Hansen's disease), a disease caused by bacteria that infect the skin and nerves. In biblical times, leprosy was thought to be a punishment from God. Those who suffered from leprosy were usually cast out of normal society.

Mantle (p. 412)

A mantle was a long sleeveless garment that resembled a cape.

The Northern Kingdom (p. 402)

After King Solomon's reign, Israel was separated into two kingdoms, the Northern Kingdom and the Southern Kingdom. The disputes between the tribes originated in King Solomon's demand that Hebrew men spend one third of their time working without pay to build his temple and palace. This aroused great anger, and after his death the northern part of the country revolted.

The Northern Kingdom, with Samaria as its capital, kept the name of Israel. It was the home of ten tribes, all but Judah and Benjamin. The Southern Kingdom, where the tribe of Judah lived, was named Judah and Jerusalem was its capital.

Peacocks (p. 400)

The peacock, the male of a bird called the peafowl, was popular in the palaces of Bible lands because of the long, colorful tailfeathers that it raises to form a beautiful fan.

Samaria (p. 402)

Omri, king of the Northern Kingdom, built a fortified city of great beauty about 40 miles from Jerusalem. It was called Samaria and became his capital.

Scribe (p. 432)

A scribe was someone who could read and write. In biblical times most people could not do either, so scribes could earn a living by using these skills. Some scribes taught reading and writing. Others, in those days before printing, made copies of the

444

Scriptures. Still others worked at the palaces of kings, copying papers and keeping records.

Sheba (p. 400)

Sheba was a very powerful kingdom in the southwestern part of the Arabian Peninsula, where modern Yemen is located. Its people, the Sabaeans, were Semites.

Syrians (p. 409)

Syria was a country north of Israel. Its capital was the beautiful and ancient city of Damascus. Although the Syrians, who were Semites, had supplied King David with war chariots, they later turned against the Hebrews.

Syria still exists, with its southwest corner at the Sea of Galilee.

The Southern Kingdom (p. 402)

After the revolt in the north (see Northern Kingdom) the southern part of Solomon's kingdom remained centered around the old capital, Jerusa-lem. It was ruled by his son Reho-boam. The Southern Kingdom was named Judah, after the tribe of Judah.

The Temple (p. 397)

Although Solomon's Temple was beautiful and richly decorated, it was modeled on Moses' simple sanctuary. Built about 950 B.C., the temple stood for almost 400 years before it was destroyed by the Babylonians.

Tishbite (p. 402)

A Tishbite was a person from Tishbe in Gilead, east of the Jordan River.

Tribute (p. 434)

A weak country was often forced to pay money to a stronger one. These payments, known as tribute, purchased peace for the weaker country.

Vassal (p. 435)

A vassal is a person who gives his loyalty and service to a stronger person in return for protection.

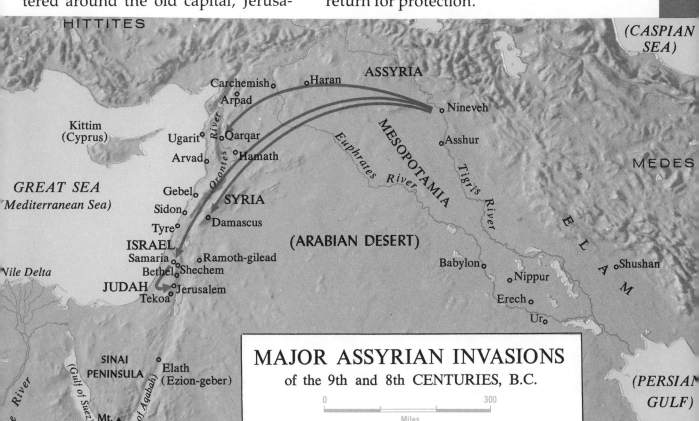

MAJOR ASSYRIAN INVASIONS
of the 9th and 8th CENTURIES, B.C.

0   300
Miles

© Copyright 1957 by Map Projects Inc.